Human Crutches
Damon Ferrell Marbut

BareBackPress

BareBackPress
Hamilton, Ontario, Canada
For enquires visit www.barebackpress.com
For information contact press@barebacklit.com
Cover layout Peter Jelen
Photography by Damon Ferrell Marbut

POEMS

This book is dedicated to the residents
of the French Quarter in New Orleans, Louisiana.

Note from the Author

The observational nature of this collection is mostly my seeking material through the confessions of others. And as usual in the French Quarter of New Orleans where I live, the environment for such divulgences is a bar. Some, though few, of these conversations are *to* myself *from* myself, whereas all others are very real, concrete and tell accidental truths about those to whom the voices and stories belong. *Human Crutches* is based on talks between bartenders, patrons, drunks on the street, and moments where sober life away from the bars collide with faces as reminder of what still lurks when the business suits come off and play begins.

It should also be noted here that I've largely held great affection for most of these "characters" and maintain correspondence with the majority of them, the exceptions being those who've passed away and those who, after too much exposure to them, eventually revealed themselves as too toxic to do anything with besides remember them and the dysfunctional living that leaked out into talks across dark bars where I worked and took a couple years' worth of mental notes.

~ Damon Ferrell Marbut

Directly From The Training Manual (1)

A good chance exists
the power will fail
and all the dripping
of water from the ceiling
will fill the shoes you bought
to work here,
and I'm sure you'll feel
at some point
you should be rewarded
for diligence
and not spat upon
by circumstance
but have you seen the folks
that come in this place?

A Network She Don't know

I'll have a gin and tonic.

He wore a scarf and specs
and there was "talk" around the bars
in text messages that *that* fucking queen
was back from South Carolina.

This time he cursed the place for not
showing CNN cover the tsunami.

Only music videos, he was told.

Eight million people died in a hot second!
And you don't care!

Even the straight bartenders said he was
made-up drama.

I'll just go somewhere else!

There really isn't anywhere here, Sally,
you can go.

Old Timer

Do me a favor,
tell that little faggot behind the bar
to get me another one of these
when he takes a break
from twirling around back there
like he's worth a shit or gonna make money
ignoring me, I know everybody who's worked here
or will work here, don't you know who I am,
I drove from Metarie
yeah
all the way here just to get another one of these
and listen, Nancy, I did my part
to get here just for this sorry lot of queers
nursing drinks all quiet in the dark,
I tell ya, there are too many twinky skinny types out now
not like the old days when real men
didn't need you to buy 'em a drink for some play,
now it's boys on their Grinders and Facebookings
acting like they deserve something,
ya heard me,
get that faggot to stop dancing
and pay attention, I coulda stayed at home
with my wife for this.

Charades

First sign the Quarter was making me heartless
was after I got past all the toughness,
I was nice a long while and then I got scared
walking home at night
and making it there in one piece
just to come to work and find out
one of my staff was sliced up from knives
and coming in late.
Way after that, I was established as someone
and people knew my name, got waved to often
when I bought groceries in the morning, that whole thing,
I was heading in one early evening,
some poor bastard was flat out on his back
while tourists took pictures of him and laughed,
I stepped over the kid and kept on for a block
before I realized I was different than before New Orleans,
had less of that old love,
so I went back and gave him my hand,
said Man, somebody's gonna take your phone
and you might end up in jail,
maybe lose your money, maybe more,
the kid said I'm fine, I can find my hotel,
it's on Canal Street
and then he pointed to the heavens
like that was where he belonged,
I said Take my arm, I'll show you.

Blood In The Bed, After

thought it was a dream/just a vision/when I came to it was/as I
suspected/leaves and limbs gone ape shit out the window/my
reflection between skin/glass/wind and all those police sirens I
could taste/a sure sign we were all breathing/grandmother air
from between lips onto abrasions/a little spit came out/wet
warnings of what not to do when drunk/like run

I Miss You Means Fuck You For Leaving

No wonder we never see you around anymore.
I couldn't tell you the last time I was under trees,
in the fall, leaves coming down over my shoulder.
Get too afraid I'd lose an eye if I turned toward the sun,
man, it's like skin cells from the world
shaking off limbs like in a bath,
can't say I like the Quarter better, but really,
where else does someone like me go?
The breeze is here, too, it's just meaner
off the bricks, pulls everything from the ground
like band-aids and mashed birds and semen and blood
and spit and broken glass, liquor from the guts of plastic cups
you used to see all the time, not like now,
too "busy" to condescend and come down
and grace us with your presence,
too good to darken a door or vomit in a trashcan anymore.
I'm sure you do it in private uptown 'cuz it's more noble,
you've got money now,
a classy lady with purpose
or a real life I never hear you mention when you pull up a seat
and say how much you miss this smell.

Can You Stay For One More

Security had to break down his door,
they said it was some sort of erotic asphyxiation,
no joke,
and this is the craziest part,
he had a baseball bat in his ass, really,
the thick end,
it kills me that people die hiding their kicks,
I'm surprised it's not in the news,
it was in a high-end hotel right across the street.

Veteran Speaks

Don't turn and look now,
but that queen in your section's been
cryin' her eyes out for an hour,
what,
yeah she does that every time she's here,
look,
let her drink all she fuckin' wants to,
ok,
that's her hag to her left,
they're both lawyers and hate the world
but somethin' tells me they either hate being home alone
or it's a real pleasure to cry on each other in public
then drop that black AMEX,
I mean,
it's none of my business
and who the hell knows,
be nearby at all times for that shit,
stupid as they are
they have money and know how to spend it,
what,
yeah it's just Absolut
but make 'em feel good, dickhead,
tell 'em they belong.

Text Message

I'm piece of shit no one will ever love me.
I'm old and fatjust wshI had
someone like you t be better than frien

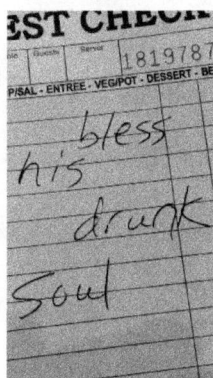

Directly From the Training Manual (2)

Look, to be completely honest
I'm over this fucking place,
have been a long time and if you make it
past three years, bravo queen,
you're as big a fucking lunatic as me,
I'm moving out of state and staying gone,
got a man who loves me in spite of all this,
look around, what's your legacy gonna be one day,
pride in yourself you survived a shift
without one of these old guys stuffing their jeans
and rubbing it against your leg
while you pass through for ice,
or you wanna tell your grandkids you figured out
how with great skill you could avoid
when the oldies find a way to get their tongues
in your mouth when you lean over to do
that friendly kiss, you don't know what I mean yet,
but watch out, those fuckers are patient,
fast, and once they get you no napkin or tequila shot
can rinse away that shame.

Loner Haiku
(String 1)

inside your poem,
a fire-warmed cottage of mind,
each ghost turns his head

off to pick up love
a few new filled-in potholes
haven't fixed a thing

perfect image of
whiskey sits bedside again
no trigger gets pulled

Barkeep(s) An Eye On The Universe

Not enough occurs
in the realm of magic.

Ringleaders wag about but
nothing is led past the bark of
sweat-belly
and
spit
and
elephants on The Net
and
the deportation of clowns.
No leader I know scrapes up shit.

Create and move on. Create and move on.

Time for more stuff to levitate.
Time for sleepers in boxcars. Just that.
Time for more sax notes and less addiction.

Time for
the center
of this house
to hold
and every
man in here
to go
back where
he's come from.

Lemme Tell You 'Bout The Janitor

(How he had time
to suck that man's dick)   ...

What   ?

And the man is married to boot   ?

Well I neva   !

I didn't see a wife around   .

(Oh yeah   ,

she's just outside the bar   .

No   ,

that one   .

Yep   ,

the one with a baby stroller   .

Oh   ,

who cares that she smokes   --

ain't there bigger fish to fry   ?)

Yes, Just Go

I can take out a row
of drinkers
stumbling outta this place,
did it few weeks ago for a birthday thing,
yeah, at some point it makes sense
to just pay my fucking tab
and stop asking myself
why are people here,
what makes them carry on.

Man of Science

The earth bulges somewhat at the belly,
about 42 miles longer a trip than if you took her
pole to pole. Word is that shape's called an ellipsoid,
or perhaps I recall geoid instead.
Maybe they're the same thing.
What I do wonder is about that 42,
times 5,280 makes 221, 760 feet in difference
from cold up to cold down
rather than hum around the warm gut.
I'd suppose Earth she can be more subtle in maternity there
in the center than all that waiting for change upon change
and two frigid payoffs. I wonder how many 12-inch belts
are ever made and how there'd ever be time
to link them together to stretch around the Congo
and Brazil and Somalia, and oddly as I sit here,
no way you or I would know
if a volcano or earthquake could shake something loose
and the planetary pants would slip right down,
who knows,
toward a cold pole if it were Man,
or Woman's water might melt and wash all our sins away.

Guess How Many Life Beans

One hundred sixty eight hours in the week
minus seventy five hours between us at work

and then subtract the fifty six we sleep
mostly side by side where he wrestles and I mumble

and let's remove the six hours he goes to meetings
to tell strange folk he's a drunk and then
there's the one hour he's up later than me and the one
I'm up earlier than him so that's twenty nine hours awake

with love on ends of the earth

I think as I sit here it's only four point one four hours per day
possible together if we make them ours
yet the number I get wrong all the time is how many cubes fit
into this thing, sir, it's empty again I'll have another.

Far Away Nearby Night

When you banged on her gate for money
and the neighbors stirred,
you yelled while she pulled her hair
and called you Fag and the cops said,
easy, use his real name.

Obsessive

I think his hair was longer.
Maybe curlier.

No, that was him
on most of the sidewalk
carrying pamphlets(?)
talking to himself like we've seen
people talk to themselves.

Almost normal these days.

It was the same man
in restaurant blacks
destined to get robbed like that
outside cafes nodding like a friend
or at least not a stranger
fixing up table tents
and walking the white traffic line
across the street
UP ON TIPTOES CAREFUL NOW
three steps to the left in good sunlight,
extract a bottle from the bush, good sir!
and scare a mom walking tots
before off toward another planned place
in the light of day.

I think he's crazy.

Now I just feel kinda bad for him.

Well, he crossed safely
didn't he(?)
He may not know what he does
but he does it and now he's gone.

You Never Can Tell

His wife turned over the boy
in Washington or Alaska and until adolescence
all seemed fine. Then a decision was made
to go to Mexico and take a crack at oblivion
and drinking again. He'd been dry a while.
He talked of those houses and walls and alleyways there
where beer was cheap twelve hours from the border.
Time went on and the boy grew up and went off to college
and the father tried to kill himself
in a stiff breeze at the edge of a canyon
but instead he liquored up in a running car.
Woke up furious in a hospital.
"I'm giving you two options," said Doc.
"Sign these papers and see a shrink, or don't sign
and we'll send you to a shrink."
Man hated it but didn't run and didn't die.
Told his son he wouldn't leave again.
Son didn't remember things like dad.
The father hunched over a podium
during a cold front in Louisiana
and spoke of thermodynamics and finished with atheism
and after the talk a couple guys approached him and said,
"Thanks for representing us heathens in the crowd" and
"There were Christians groaning at first but even they
all applauded at the end."
The father, maybe thinking to himself,
I'm just a broken Dad on the mend, said,
"Did you notice me hesitate? I thought for a minute not to go
there."

If The River Rose Today

No
I won't leave the bed
it's got nice sheets
and pillows marked with sweat of strangers
I will not leave bed yet
to turn right out of the gate
then right down Royal
after doing all that looking down
in stormy weather or ignorant sun
I won't
I'm not putting down a foot
that makes this all happen
that makes me shove on past the play yard
where my friend was hired and fired
I still have paint on my shorts from helping
just to go back to work
me
to go back to the bar
and stand there and say
you may have another
god help me
the words sound like rape feels
but the faucet drip from the sink
sounds like honesty because it's real
no
I won't leave the bed until it's time.

Dignity

The boy came in crying,
his face a knotted mass
revolting against sunlight
and the long walk he took
with a meth dealer he'd been
warned about, time and again,
and a cop was with him,
the dealer as well.
They were all talking over one another.
They were all so removed from the lives
of artists and corporate winners,
just stale souls on the concrete visiting motions.
At some point all involved were kids,
not on Bourbon Street in the heat.
Once it seems each took on a different innocence
and its absence was like bad fathers in that it was gone,
whatever was similar in their old potential.
A nose was busted,
a lie was told,
someone was pleading and the cop
was fed up and uncaring.
No one was tugged in by a sleeve.
Barkeep said he didn't know the story
and wiped away an ash with a towel.
Murder was so close in the afternoon.
The boy said to no one he just wanted his satchel,
he was homeless in town from Michigan,
trusted wrong and didn't choose right,
said breakfast was a glass pipe and all his earth was stolen.
Cop asked again what anyone knew
and the dealer shook his head,
the boy balled a fist and said he'd suck a dick for train fare.
He didn't say that but his tears meant it.
A tranny limped in on a broken heel
and they all went quiet to watch.

Loner Haiku
(String 2)

the ol' switcheroo—
clock hand plays "pull my finger,"
a drunk sighs "tick-tock"

downstairs is quiet
see who's sad twenty steps up
yours motherfucker

old spool, heavy heart,
pens that will not piss out ink,
the list goes on and

We Will Always Live Forever

1.

You mean I never told you
the story about when I hung out with Delta Burke,
girl, she was fun and honey lemme tell ya
she could slug back them Long Islands
when she wanted to, and of course you know
I only drink wine, but honey back in those days
when I was doin' my young drinkin'
it was everything I could get my hands on,
and hell even at this bar, I musta worked here off and on now
maybe going on fifteen, twenty *years*,
I was known from time to time to sit back there
and just tie one on, *mercy*, and try to get up and outta here
and one time, are you sure I never told you this one,
I was proppin' myself up against that cash register,
well not *that* one, back then we had them old heavy clunkers,
yeah, where you could hear 'em clickin',
and girl I tried to push off that thing walkin' out
and somehow managed to pull it instead
back on top of myself, dragged it right down to the ground,
and honey lemme tell ya
it got quiet as a church whisper in here
until my drunk little head popped up all smiles
and they sent my happy ass off to bed.

2.

I don't see
why you're leaving.
You waitin' for
me to say
Don't go?
I'd go crazy if I had to live
with *my* mother again.

3.

Well hello there *doll*!
I can't explain enough
how good it is to see ya,
say,
we need to have another sit-down at the studio,
wear everything or next to nothing,
it don't matter,
just wouldn't mind having that kind face of yours around,
man oh *man*,
I wasn't told *you'd* be at this little soiree.

4.

Well it's always a struggle,
in the end and when nothing much else matters
and you let the body go
but keep on top of the mind.
That's what I do.
I disappear long enough,
go hunt for spaces in which to burrow,
die a little,
come back to life, repeat.
Most of ya'll around here call it returning to reality,
but come on, now. *Really*?
When the fuck did anyone *we* know ever leave?

5.

Hey!
If I see you still working here in ten years
I'll have *zero* respect for you!
You know why?
I didn't piss my thirties away
and neither should you.
I'm a real live motherfucker!

6.

I
just
like
to
sip
my
diet
coke
and
watch
people
from
the
sidelines.

7.

Sweetie,
I'm already an old queen,
I mean, look at me.
And look at these Marys around here
freakin' out when I shave
like I've done something wrong.
I'm fine with being a snooty bear
and having my cocktail in peace.
It doesn't help that I hate everyone
and I'm proud of having no soul, or at least,
not enough of one to make black paint stick.
What?
He said I was into fisting?
Uh huh. Just wait and see.
I'ma kill that sonofabitch.

8.

During the day I wear a suit.
I'm sure you hear that all the time.
God knows what you see in this place,
or what you believe from these cock-stuffed mouths.
See I don't go out any other day than Sunday,
ya heard? It's the only day I *can*
and keep living my "respectable" life.
Notice my quotations.
But as it goes, sure, you might see me
on the streetcar in the mornings.
Don't worry. You don't have to say Hi.
I don't need the acknowledgment.
Matter of fact it's good we keep things as they are.
You're my bartender.
I mean it when I say this,
'cuz what do I have to lose?
I would *love* to eat your ass.

9.

I know,
that's probably stuff you don't like,
but I love it.
I met a porn star at one of those parties.

You probably don't wanna hear this,
but his penis was tasty.
It was so weird, too.
Not his penis, but how shy he was.

I guess when the cameras are rolling, right?

10.

The funny thing is
they still keep coming in here together
like nothing's wrong.
Like nobody sees when they fight.
I remember you told me
they were hitting each other
last Valentine's.

One night I heard all this yelling outside
and no one was in here so I walked out
and they were across the street by Pat's place
and Billy had Sean pinned up against the wall
and was just slamming his head against it
and Sean was screaming for him to stop
and I almost went out there and broke it up.

But whaddya do?
Have 'em hate you for knowing the truth?
Gotta make a dollar somehow.

11.

He left me because I don't have any money.
I came to New Orleans with some,
but not a lot.
He just always wanted what he had growing up,
somebody to take care of him
like he can't or won't himself.
And it hurt pretty bad.
I started back with photography
because I needed pretty things
more than I realized before.
When he came back to me I realized also
that he wasn't coming back, per se.
I'd been saving up and so I said *Come on*.

Night Haiku
(String 1)

dark is obvious —
it is Alaska somewhere
and all around cold

                   maybe she's not night
                 maybe she's mother nature
                     turned over, a whore

"imagine a frost"
(instructions given my throat)
what else now but wait

42

Once It Was Called "Gay Cancer"

Girl,
I talk alotta shit
but really
this is what's going down,
I already told Tom
and I might as well tell you,
I need to tell somebody else here,
there was a scare
if you know what I mean,
I got fucked up
and made a bad choice,
just sayin' motherfucker didn't tell me
until after,
so I went to my doctor
and she gave me these pills
that make me sick as fuck,
for now,
it's why you're gonna see me puking
here this week,
maybe a few days,
I dunno,
I'll tell you the results when I know,
but if you see me disappear
from behind the bar
without sayin' why,
cover my ass and when I come back out
tell me if I got something on my face.

Gone Blues

(The Lights Are On)

It's really sad to see the good ones go,
sure he still comes around
but if you saw his face all that nothingness
has taken over, he used to hang out at Bill's bar
but I don't think he can make it,
even for dementia he had his alert days
and now when he comes in his face is heavy,
more wrinkled, everything looks more lost
even though I still hear in his voice that niceness
he had more control of as little as a year ago
before he'd slip off into the bathroom
and get caught giving out handies,
these days he gets the same drink,
only stays for one long one,
a glass of wine and always a cup of ice with it,
which he never uses, just dumps it out on Baronne
then comes back in, holy shit,
yesterday he walked outside and tossed the ice
right into the window of a Mercedes,
I mean, one look at the old boy now,
how mad could they really get?

(He Won't Know You But He's Kind)

Yeah,
he's from a line of political royalty,
I'm not sayin' who
but it's money, more than you or I got,
his dementia's kicked in and he can make it around some,
comes in sometimes with scrapes from the sidewalks
where he fell, you know,
but nothing ever seems to happen to those rings,
tens of thousands of dollars on his fingers
and he's walkin' around with a cape and cane,
I didn't take him seriously for a long time,
just thought he was an old bat like normal
but there's a sweet side to him when he's clearheaded which,
trust me, ain't every day,
more times than not he'll get a bourbon and coke
put on top of a chardonnay and sprite,
and he's barely got cash, I think some guy handles his shit,
I met him once, meant to ask him why he was letting
this lost old man give strangers hand jobs in the bathroom
but I wimped out and took his business card instead.

Can't Take Off The Fatigues

What caused it?
Me yelling on the street and tryin' to kill people?
I'm diagnosed bipolar disorder and PTSD
and I'm not supposed to be doing this,
not supposed to have a drink at all,
you know,
I do the best I can for her,
rub her feet when she gets home
and I cook her dinner, man,
I tell her any way I can that she's loved,
but I'm fucked up
and when it's not mania
it's depression,
I don't know why I'm sayin' all this,
I'm sick as fuck and haven't slept for days,
is it cool I'm in here even though I'm straight?
I worked in a gay bar once.
Good money
but it was hell.

A Thing Or Two About A Thing Or Two

Sure
he tips five bucks when he wins
and even buys a coke to stay
but "they" say it's huge
and he only fucks raw.

Damn right
that kid looks like all the others
always playing on their phones
ready to split when the poker slots quit or—
yes, really—
mom "goes out for the night"
so junior can bring home the lad
and have something to text about later
when the cock crows.

Lady Dusk

Most people don't know I'm a reader,
I mean, look at me and can'tcha tell?
My goddamn teeth fall out when I get mad
and these cape codders don't go down without help
at least I call 'em cape codders, I mean,
don't get me wrong I love these people
and the work's not bad but sometimes I just like
sittin' alone back here alone even though the music's
too loud, and of course people know me well enough
to come say Hi, I'm not sure why I'm telling you all this,
it ain't like you're not busy as hell, I follow you on Facebook,
I told you I read your novel? It was good, I mean that,
I tell everybody, and I know you're way uptown
away from here and livin' some kind of fantasy,
well darlin' it ain't *my* dream but you know what I mean,
and it gets lonely down here more than you know,
especially since you left, and my husband's back from rehab
and that, I'm sure you remember,
makes me all kinds of nervous
but it is just so good to see you, I'm sorry I'm crying,
it's just been one of those days, you know,
and *whatever*, I lived your new kind of life once upon a time,
we owned our own business but his drinkin' took over
and now look at me, wonderin' if you grow jasmine like I did
or love your husband like I don't, I miss the way it was,
mm-hmm, go ahead and make your rounds,
forget I said I liked your book, it's fine, I get it.

Retired From The Scene

I used to work there, too,
don't need to date myself
but it was ages ago,
had a nice, trim body,
made a lot of money, it was fun,
helped me start my construction company,
now I'm a fat old queen
with heart problems and nine lawyers,
I look back at those days
and just thank God I made it out alive,
saw too, too many people come and go,
oh, killed off by one thing or another,
I don't make it to the Quarter much anymore
'cuz why would I,
not looking for a date,
not like anyone would have me,
besides no matter how many good souls I knew
it was easy enough to make enemies,
all you had to do
was seem happy in all that filth.

What We Learned And What We Invented

They said Tennessee Williams was here
and you wanted to move to Nashville

then They told us Capote drank right there
in that chair
and you got reminiscent about Kansas
or maybe that was me
and you just said something about Spain

before They said
this is an eternal flame
of some sort or another
and you looked away as I watched the door man
eject a fool who blew it out
and gas smell went everywhere

and when you returned from that apathy
They were waiting for one of us to be dazzled
you told Them sorry and that you'd not listened

and I said
That's some kind of story
I think the world should burst in flames

to the consternation of a brow or two
and just on the tips of Their tongues
an accusation   as if to say
we were out of place and didn't belong
and since we were there it was best to pretend
than let our minds wander

or better yet
best not to bring minds at all.

Directly From The Training Manual (3)

Keep a bar towel nearby
for that one,
he twitches like a motherfucker
and he's gonna ash all around the ashtray
but never in it,
talk your fuckin' ear off, too,
but he won't hit on you
and I think he comes from money,
no fuckin' way he delivers pizza
and affords that Cadillac outside,
yeah that black shiny one
gettin' pissed on.

Know What I Mean

I meant to tell ya, sweetheart,
the last time I saw you
I was outta my mind, been drinking all day,
and you know it started as laundry,
the weather was nice, my father called from Milwaukee,
no, it wasn't as bad as I thought it would be,
we said a couple nice things
and I went out after,
the laundry smelled so good through the house,
I didn't know I'd be that smashed when I saw you
or that you'd even be out,
you know I never told you I was sorry
for doing that big dick contest upstairs where you work,
I got second place and put the prize money
back into your bar.

Night Haiku
(String 2)

from the porch it's clear
young boys on the street assume
control comes from balls

a scream, a whimper
<u>details</u> if a "good neighbor"
and cops are not called

jazz man over lamp,
the glow's forgiving orange,
no sunset HE knew

What Isn't Said Here

Gladness has a light
around it
that seems so numbing
a porcupine could storm through,
enraged,
and not one quill
could pierce the bubble
or be a wind
that breaks the fog.

He Will Rest In Peace

Didn't realize it/you were sad from loss/I was thinking of you
on the streetcar/hit Poydras and something changed/wanted to
get out and run to you/but a bad knee/you know the rest/hell
you got me a job because of your bad feet/oh those were the
days/getting drunk at five in the morning/not drunk as adults
fighting off smiling faces still lingering in the bars/my god we're
getting old/you didn't respond with too many words/that small
brown bar and your usual seat/I blew in like I'd been shoved
inside by the earth/you waited until I reached you to begin to
cry/I loved you for that/It's really hard--you told my chest--I
can still hear the old bastard call me a motherfucker

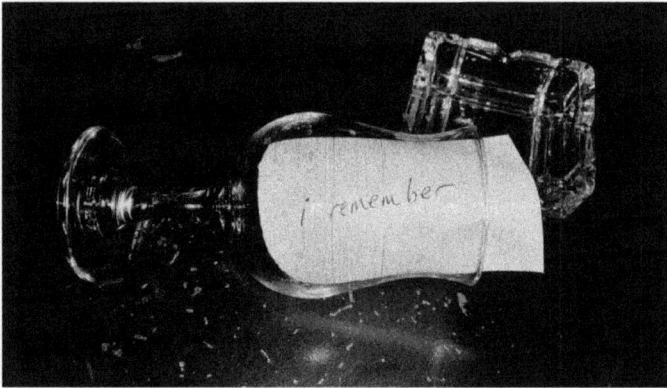

"Right Now I Am Happy"

It's not that he's talking about the drink,
shit,
I've made a thousand of those,
maybe more and probably more
if I counted back,
he might be glad the dust is out of his mouth
from decades of telling stories
that worked against him,
he's a cute, cuddly little man,
but his type is dangerous, too,
a guy like him smiled all the time
and came into my bar one rainy night
way before I lived here,
I set out his Perrier and Crown rocks,
he wouldn't look me in the face,
I said,
Hey Mr. Beale,
he said,
this is the kinda weather
where you should be at home
curled up with somebody's dick between yer legs,
I think
the older they get the less they plan on losing.

Big Man Says Give Up The Life

That's what we get?
From preachers and the revered,
oh man,
human connection is a butterfly
and a lily pad, ok,
I wanna decorate the world with glow sticks
and tears,
but when it comes to God
I'm better off accepting the whip
from outside sugarcane,
earth hurts, and fuckin' A,
I didn't live this long
shut down by a voice upstairs
just to be all right with it,
shit,
if God doesn't love me because I'm sad
in this world
what good did he do, ever,
even my straight friends tell me
we got the worst kinda deal.

Why We Don't Heal

Nobody wants
to talk
to the
devil's advocate.

In Secret I Was With You

This is going to sound nuts
I realize
but since I never said it until now
that I have always been in love with you
I should also say I followed you one night
out of that Bywater bar
we'd run into each other
remember
I was with my husband
of oh I don't know how long now
and you were upset
I could tell later but not then
as you sat at the bar and smiled at everyone
like you do
I never saw until then how lonely you are
behind it
it was cold for December
and Christmas was in hours
you were drunk as I've seen
and talking to yourself
the streets were so quiet
beyond laughter more toward the city
you stopped to piss and leaned into a phone pole
your shoulder kept slipping off it
and you were crying
I thought for a minute you would hurt yourself
but you stayed up
you stood well enough
and kept telling   God I wish it was me
you kept telling someone in the dark
how much you wished you could talk.

Lawyer, Mr. Teeth

Sit your hurt body down, there's room for you
and those Marlboros of your smile
hanging just too rigid to dangle
and your hands so shook up I light your teeth,
watch them burn skyward to the nubs.

You grin awake in vapors of vodka perfume.

In your short spiked hair   I see   a long blonde strand
from a Golden Retriever—she stares at the door, sad.

You mention sometimes how she waits for you like that.

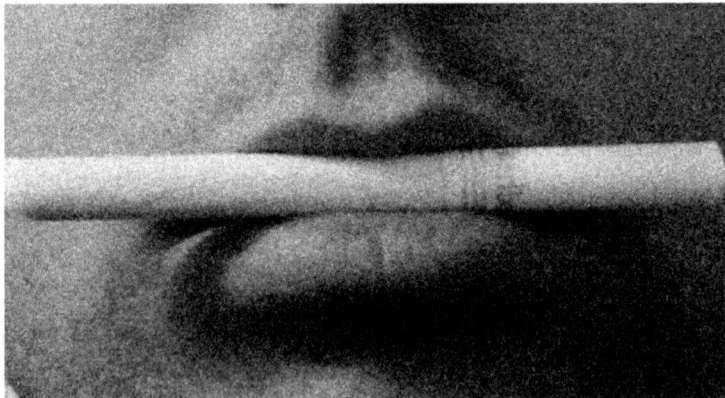

There Should Be A Law

I'd just as soon cut off my feet
than walk around here barefoot,
you see all those gutter punks begging for change,
oh hell yes it's a business, a fucking game,
all that olive drab, stringing along sick looking dogs,
ain't no cop gonna mess with that,
just tell 'em to move it on along
when a tourist gets bitten or a fat cat in dreadlocks
with some trust fund from Vermont
calls anyone a faggot for not handing over a sandwich,
or maybe it's dollars they're after, if it's a real business,
but how much do you think they really make
to cover the shards and sticks climbing up into their feet,
I read a puncture is less mess but still allows in the germs,
honestly, it's in your fucking skin so I'm sure
we're sending half of them to Tulane medical on our dime,
and even when they wear sandals and do yoga in the park
it's all an act, look at us we're peaceful and tan,
fuck that,
I'd rather be a pale face in here drinking what I earn.

Star Haiku
(String 1)

I was alone some
then exchanges occurred while
I slept, undreamt of

"nebula" was good,
then thoughts of the Milky Way
changed how I saw words

just because I drift
and for whatever reason
I am born again

My Girl

It's peculiar, no doubt,
that we'll walk together down Burgundy
and across the Quarter to the movies,
him in heels and done up nice
and me in a hoodie I read in a recent article
indicates I've not grown up,
and people talk to themselves aloud
about his boots, which I admit look good,
not my face that ages faster than his,

he's so bad with directions
I forget until we're where I used to live
on Barracks Street alone, but even when
I drove him around my childhood homes
it had been hours in the car and while his eyes were shut
he stayed less argumentative because it meant something to
me,

like days of false winter here
on the sidewalks,
and stopping at our usual place,
we both have to piss and bicker over
who's to hold a place in line,

and then the food comes and we cheer up,
he hears that sigh of mine
that we're off schedule and I let it go
because even I know what I'm doing,
we leave the restaurant and walk across the street
to get tickets,
he makes a joke that I'm not listening
(as if either of us do after these years)
I want to tell him I had a dream two nights prior,
same as the usual visions
that come like worry,
how I have to keep him safe and close

no matter how pretty the shoe,
how impossible the man,
even when *I'm going to leave you*
isn't what I mean, ever,
yet still it's said.

Rings On A Tree

Oh, he'll tell everyone it's his birthday,
he comes in announcing himself anyway
so what's another day of it,
he got older and he champions himself
and talks of his penis and how he
"speaks the Queen's English"
but by the end of the night
he's stolen someone's heartbreak
by promising them weed and his "monster",
he got rolled so many times by druggies
and limped in here from the hospital,
of course he blamed the city,
and granted, I love the guy,
but what's there left to say when
everyone's got a birthday around here
and are quieter about it,
here's to getting on another day,
but in fairness he did say one thing to me
that stuck long after he left the bar,
he said,
a poem can fight for its own life.

Boss Gives A Speech On Domestic Partnership

Oh,
I'm fit to be tied,
been in a mood all damn day
and now I gotta be at this shithole
all night long,
Rick started his shit again
banging on my goddamn door,
yes, at four in the fucking morning,
I haven't slept for shit
'cuz I talked to the cheatin' muthafucka
through the door,
hell no I didn't let 'im in,
that *bitch*, after the money I given 'im
and his ol' worthless ass too good to work,
I'm knuckles to the fuckin' bone around here
just to have a lyin' triflin' sonofabitch
wakin' my ass at all hours of night,
shit, it ain't like he's had a hard time
findin' another bed before,
I'm just pissed as hell, that's all,
already had me two Long Islands
and this is my third,
they can fire me all I care,
it's gonna take somethin' stiffer than this
to make things right.

The Man Who Fell Down The Stairs

Yours was the biggest heart,
a grin as wide as a Harley
and just as loud. Everyone saw your picture
after you were buried between flower petals
on the river and went adrift.
No one remembers if barges pressed on
or made that wide turn east and swung a big rump out
near the shore before righting itself and moving on.
The "preacher" was maybe your family thing,
and it was doubted they knew he was a dick sucker
and drank too much brown liquor. A man most thought
hated you was in tears, those good quiet ones that roll
and have no sound. Someone who looked like a secret poet
was in shambles and two kids showed up late
in the sun looking pristine for you.
All those late hours, darling.
My God.
The bankruptcy of it.
Human crutches propping you up
toward the bathhouse
and telling that cunt at the window
to get you down on a bed but, first and foremost,
make sure you were breathing.

Heard His Body Hadn't Even Cooled

It isn't fair to call it plain old drama,
which is what it was,
but nobody around here's gonna react the same
when it comes to someone else dying,
especially a loved one,
and for some reason a power struggle
popped up this time
like death wasn't enough pain

but yeah, you heard pretty much what I know,
they were throwing things across the bar
and smashing stuff, people were crying
and a lot of regulars just paid out and left,
you'd think planning a funeral would be easy enough
around the tears, but who knows,
it isn't the last death on earth,
they'll eventually come to their senses
once they realize
the thing you can always give away
but never lose is hurt.

Driver Says Take A Day

Tell him no,
say you can't fucking work today, queen,
I didn't drag you all the way to the Westbank
for costumes just to have you bail on me,
the lo mein is on the way, fatass,
big surprise we'd eat twice or shop this long,
quit being the bigger man,
that company ain't hangin' on your word you'll show,
and just look at this thing,
old fuckin' Nissan,
you wanna try and power through the toll bridge
to throw on pants and ask those fags for dollars,
I didn't think so,
I'm still laughing on the inside about eating in the mall
with you, we're such drunks, you can tell,
they said we forgot our drinks at the counter
and I ran off like it was cocktails gettin' drugged.

Run A Tab, I Got Clean

You know, kid,
you're older than me
and were a doctor a while.
I'm glad you've come full circle
with the drinking
and recall the last time you were in here
kissing up my arm at 4 a.m.
You were talking how gross it is
to help a woman give birth.

You missed my point.

I imagine the scent of you
hovering over her body,
insisting on drugging her for pain
sweating beer over her vagina
as that kid came into the world
screaming about how warm it once was,
how cold your fingers were against its skin
and the lasting impression of a father's eyes
on your shoulder, saying without saying,
hey, have we met somewhere?

We're All Thinking It

Dis jus' me
wishin' God
put his big ol'
outstretched palm
down in the earth
and make her heart beat better
or hell
for Christmas
just push this city
up a few feet.

Breaking News

Girl, I was just down on Bourbon
having my first, and honey,
some drunk bitch came wheelin' in the bar
and yellin' over the speakers
We got Bin Laden! We got Bin Laden!
and you know I can't hear good
outta this ear anyway,
and some folks by the door started clapping
while Derek, you know him,
the cute one who writes poems,
he shrugged his shoulders like she was crazy,
'cuz really, who knows if we got the motherfucker
and who knows what anybody's got comin' to 'em,
hell,
it was my first cocktail, honey,
no time for that shit,
some lady screamin' 'bout what we don't know,
I wanted to say, *Honey, that's everything!*
but my voice ain't up to it
and the night's so young.

Star Haiku
(String 2)

give me back prowess,
if that's ever possible—
shining gets so old

was that your front porch?
all of that skyward gazing,
my dick in your plants

a plane between us,
mouths never thinking of me
order more pretzels

They Call *Her* The Chalmatian

Oh girl
who *hasn't* had her,
she got a nice dick
but lawd knows she from the *parish*
tryin' make sunthin' of herself,
shit,
used to put that hard thing in hands for dollaz,
ol' fatties used to call her a dick dancer
and look, now she livin' large,
got a kid's *pawty* business...

This I Got From Rehab

Consider all we can do now
that we couldn't do while drinking,
as a sort of spiritual event or awakening,

it takes a very long time to truly believe
things are and will be better
without taking another drink,

plus,

emotional sobriety
=
not reacting like a drunk while sober,

among other things.

Many have to hear something
a thousand times to first hear it.

Gay Pride Weekend Journal

Now, I know the newspapers and Facebook
tomorrow will tell me they're out there saying,

Repent now Sodomites!
The wrath of God is swift
and shall fall upon all ye who root like pigs in sin!
Fags shall burn in Hell!
You are an abomination
and your poisonous blood like snake venom
will seep into the earth and from it shall there grow
black dead orchids as reminder of the ugly life
you live!
Matthew Shepard in Hell!
God hates the military for fighting for your rights
to lay with each other!
God is love and he wants you to die!

but what I really hear is a cry for help,
someone needs a drink,
but I'm guessing the pastor would have to sign off on that,
fat fucking chance, right sweetie,
oh, I don't know why these queens get mad and run out there,
it's just misguided people doing their lord's work,
hey, I wouldn't wanna hold those heavy signs
and walk them around this place,
besides, why get up and lose a warm seat,
according to those cunts he doesn't like me
but Lord knows I'd spill my cocktail going out there
just to scream *We Don't Hate You.*

Directly From The Training Manual (4)

He's a millionaire
and gets drunk as shit
when he's out,
probably gonna try to suck your fingers,
once he likes you he tries
to hold your hand,
and he'll stare at you, no idea why,
just remember his drink
and the fact he'll make fun of people
in your section
if they don't tip you,
a good guy to have around
if you can look past the saliva
and how it stays on you.

Know It All

Everybody leaves here
but comes back in time
whether it's online
or in moments of longing,
I don't know the draw
let alone why I stay,
laziness I guess,
or maybe that I had a dream
for myself
and came here to make it real,
it's a third act city
waiting to be written,
it's a play no one gets credit for
until long after they're gone.

Today I'm Just Laughing With The World

My sister's in the hospital
this time for good
and after all this time
of all people my shrink even said
Jim Let Her Go You've Done What You Can
and I'm thinking
it's the best news I can get
from someone I'm paying that kind of money
right
so I leave Kenner and come back to my place
you know
I'm still at that apartment just down Dumaine
and so of course after a day of saying my goodbyes
and the hell of her thinking I was burying her alive
as they closed the doors between us
my fucking parking spot was taken
I don't know
by some asshole with New York plates
my old stomping grounds
and so here I am on my third double vodka
glad you're coming on shift
'cuz as coincidence has it
I just found out in Manhattan cigarettes are 15.00
and since I live here now
and my crazy sister isn't mine to hold anymore
I've got plenty of cash to drink that thought away
ha
for now at least until it gets messy
and you tell me like you've told me before
Jim cross the street and get yourself a sandwich
and from there just keep fucking going.

From Algiers

I was a patient from time to time
at various clinics around the country,
everyone knew, well, everyone that mattered
like my partner, my kids,
I never kept much from my kids
besides my partner
but then when they were old enough
or when they were what I thought to be old enough
and I came out then there was nothing to keep,
our bonds were strong, they *are* strong,
I stopped going to the doctors,
began figuring things on my own,
moved to New Orleans just across the river
and ferry over sometimes, bus often as well,
I never told you this but I think you're smart to the point
you can see on your own that I am so lonely,
so lonely, it's been almost a year now since he passed
and I don't think a minute about what's next,
what's to come, I think of how he and I used to
keep our back door unlocked, all the time,
back at our old place, for any of our friends
who needed to escape what was eating them alive,
even if it was to come smoke a few cigarettes
or come inside, hell, make a sandwich,
I was that kind of people back then
when I was half of us.

Boy Tells Boy, 3:42 a.m.

"If I were better
at telling you how
disappointing I am
then I wouldn't need you."

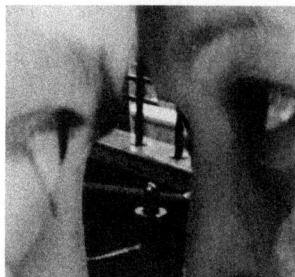

Love Is In The Air

No one else here is breaking their backs
to solve the problem of those heavy eyes,
how you wave that empty cup in the air
like a solution will land at the bottom
and rise up to explain itself to you, look,
your lover left and everyone knows he was young
as in young enough to be your son
and because no sin here is worse than the other
no one's gonna judge you overtly
so buck up you miserable bastard,
quit telling everyone you're forty-something
when you look like a dead sixty,
and come to think of it, your little lover
of old he ain't so little, a towering pre-collegiate,
and he was in here bumming coffee come six a.m.
not too long ago just after shift change
and the cleaning lady came in early,
your boy snuck upstairs to a pool table and spread out
(I'm sure you know what I mean)
and when she found him she didn't think of you,
she said get out, there's work to be done.

Star Haiku
(String 3)

gas doesn't scare me,
nor do all the telescopes
watching me explode

little bit of earth,
I want to be your father
but I'm so far gone

unstable as hell,
already labeled by god—
why pay to name me?

Streetcar Therapy, Christmas

"Well, I agree that's the toughest part
about maintaining a relationship when one person is an addict
and the other isn't, or at least isn't that kind,
since I think we all to some extent have a thing we obsess over
in a sick way we can't manage, of course,
it's been a long-gone age and a half
between now and my former lover
but I don't guess it's much a difference anyhow,
and who's to say keeping the thing goin's the best idea
when you're cleaning yourself up(?),
I'm certainly no sort of judge or jury,
but I could tell the other night something wasn't right with you
and I wanted to see if you were ok,

what, it's a free fucking country,
miss thing, we were sitting here first...(bitch)...

you know, maybe that's all there is to it,
no love at all let alone between two people,
take that cunt for example and I know I'm being awful,
it's this goddamn time of year, I can't say it's work though it *is*,
and it's not like I wanna take a drink, hell,
it's been twenty-two years since me and the wagon
took turns as boss, I dunno,
that could be the problem and hence the solution,
his lacks light and your heart is still gold."

Cocktail Hour Is A Tribunal

I wouldn't begrudge the common street trash
that came in to some money,
well, except for Bob,
his gutter name in the seventies was Tyson,
used to blow cabbies for rides around the city,
well his lover died outta nowhere
and left him a pot of gold, he bought some places
as cover for his cocaine racket, yep,
put cameras in the bathrooms of bars
to watch the deals, he's still around
and fallin' offa bar stools,
nobody's gonna miss that mean ol' asshole,

and come to think of it,
not that Baton Rouge pair either,
old gaudy rings on their fat fingers,
all HE does is talk and talk about money
while SHE sits and sometimes says,
You're being rude, they go back and forth,
and old drag queens who didn't get killed off
in the eighties stand around them glowing
and fighting to buy 'em a round, yes,
drag queens spending money, imagine that.

Maybe When The Devil Comes

Maybe sin will give itself a better name,
so all us rambunctious from fever
and the hype of promised love
will know the world's end and begin to dance,

maybe the clop of mule hooves
and drunks swan-divin' into streets gonna
take pause as the skies come down from the dark,

maybe you walk into a bar late one night
and ain't no one there but dust come up
from some explosion, some kidnapping of Grace
with angels left to tell a story on stools
unattended by floor maids and barkeeps of the air,

maybe there's gonna come a power,

maybe there will be a light,

maybe a pin prick in the doll of your heart's gonna
revive us all, animals we be,
and Earth collapses at the cackle of the wind
pitching back so forceful in God's mouth
that none of us, not even the faithful,
knew she had titties or imagination or a plan.

About the Author:

Damon Ferrell Marbut is author of the critically-acclaimed novel *Awake in the Mad World* and the Amazon bestselling collection of poetry *Little Human Accidents: Chaos Poems From The Brink*. He lives in New Orleans, Louisiana. Stay connected with Damon at www.facebook.com/DamonFMarbut

© Larry Graham

Also by the Author

Awake in the Mad World

Little Human Accidents:
Chaos Poems from the Brink

www.barebackpress.com

www.ingramcontent.com/pod-product-compliance
Lightning Source LLC
Chambersburg PA
CBHW060339050426
42449CB00011B/2796